This book is dedicated to my grandmother:

Dorothy Shelton

Table of Contents

Part 1: Love

Food is Love..1
Backwards Love..3
All-Nighter..4
Again..5
Us..6
My Love for You...7
Today's Perfection..8
Complexity...9
Sweet Tooth..10
Crazy...11
Timeless Love...12
Brand New..13
Is Love...14
For Now..15
My Ending..16
Best With You...17
Believe...18
Bring Me Back..19
I Didn't See it Coming..20
Armor..21
Perfect...23

Part 2: Life
Untraditional...24
Hold Your Opinion..25
Never Be the End..26
Color Blind..28
Once Lived..29
A Book Called Perfect..31
America..32
Sees Me..33
Disappointments...34
The Part of Me..35
Consequences..36
Jasmine...37
Bittersweet...38
So Easy...39
Nothing More..40
Insatiable..41
Mirror, Mirror..42
Progress..43
Crabs in a Barrel 45
Oya...46
If Tomorrow Doesn't Come..47
Myself...48
Footsteps..49
Just Your Taste..50
I Capture My Beauty..51
Be a Magnet...52
Everybody Knows...54
Hate to Love You..55
Comfort..57
Diamonds and Pearls..58
Order My Steps...59
This is All I Need..60
Little Old Me...61

Part 3: Family
Have You Ever Been a Kid..62
Its All for a Reason..63
My Grandmother..65
Always...66
25th Anniversary..69
A Newborn Mother...71
I Just Can't Tell it All 72

Love

Food is Love

I want to thank you
because when I first learned how to cook,
and I made you a meal
you ate it, and you smiled, and you said it was good
and it made me feel good,
because I knew my food wasn't

We both know that
the chicken was burnt
and the corn was cold
and the macaroni was too cheesy
and the greens didn't have no seasoning
and the sweet tea wasn't sweet enough
but still, my food was good enough for you
and I thank you
because that's exactly what I call love

So when I got a little older
and my food got a lot better
it was funny to see
how many people came flocking to me
so I made them a plate
and they ate it and they smiled
and they said it was good
but I didn't interpret that as love
didn't make me feel good
because I knew my food was
that so called love wasn't for the chef
but for the food
for the first time in my life
I saw how it felt to be used

Because even if
my chicken was burnt
or my corn was cold
or my macaroni was too cheesy
or my greens didn't have no seasoning
or my sweet tea wasn't sweet enough
My food still would have been good enough for you
and I thank you
because that's exactly what I call love

So when I didn't have any food
not even to feed myself
With my food left everybody else
And you, my friend, were the only one left
So you made me a plate
And I ate it, and I smiled, and I said it was good
Because it was
and I thank you
because that's exactly what I call love

And even if your
chicken was burnt
or your corn was cold
or your macaroni was too cheesy
or your greens didn't have no seasoning
or your sweet tea wasn't sweet enough
Your food still would have been good enough for me

So whether my food is good or not, cooked or not
seasoned, sweetened or not
all of my food, all of my love
will only be made for you

Backwards Love

You for is love my backwards how see you can't.
Can't you see how backwards my love is for you?

Sense makes everything where,
together somewhere away run lets.
Let's run away somewhere together
where everything makes sense.

Clear always aren't words
your and me confuse actions your sometimes.
Sometimes your actions confuse me and your
words aren't always clear.

Love backwards, my always. You Love I but.
But I love you, always, my backwards love.

All-Nighter

I'm an all-nighter, traffic light fighter
getting to my baby
but they say he's just a liar
and my speed going higher
my car getting lighter
but everyone says he's just a liar

I'm an all-nighter
greyhound bus rider
come to the city and drive right by you
going to the house, stay on the other side of
town, I'm staying with my baby
but everyone says he's just a liar

I'm an all-nighter, airplane flyer
baggage claim denier
liquid, gel supplier
boarding the plane just to see my baby
and I don't give a damn if you think he just a liar

Again

Giving in to my desire,
burning in forbidden fire
filled with such a rich sensation,
tortured by your sweet temptation
in your arms, again

Releasing all the burning passion,
taking back renewed attraction
calling me near,
aggressive confidence of no fear
in your arms, again

I feel the smooth seductive skin,
unleashing all I've kept within
a warm invasion running deep,
releasing screams from beneath
in your arms, again

I lay defeated
the act of lust, repeated
my lost addiction, recreated
coming from a long hiatus
in your arms, again

Us

You see, I loved us just as much as us loved you
and for a second, I thought you loved us, too.

I wanted us to last
not while it lasted
or when it lasted
or if it lasted
just last

I wanted us to be
not together
not apart
not even forever
just be

I wanted us to indulge
not in each other
or life or love
just indulge
in happiness
that's all
I ever wanted
was us

You see, I loved us just as much as us loved you
and for a second, I thought you loved us, too.

My love for you

The confusion of my love, for you
The unfamiliar pain of a broken heart
The uncertainty of unconditional
The exhaustion of resentment
The disgust of betrayal
The dysfunction of rage

The agony of my love, for you
The desperation of intimacy
The misguidance of romance
The standard of satisfaction
The persuasion of depression
The conquest of seduction
The addiction of my love, for you

Today's Perfection

He holds my body, caters to my toes
squeezes my belly, and loves my rolls
massages my shoulders, and rubs my feet
Today, he fell in love with every piece of me

He pinches my cheek, tickles my sides
whispers in my ear, and kisses the lids of my eyes
pecks the tips of my fingers, and holds my hand
Today, he is the perfect man

Complexity

There is nothing more complex
than life… or love
or falling in love with
your best friend's man
or your man's best friend
or your best male friend

But I am
with or without you
free from complexity

There's nothing more complex
than life… or love
or falling in love for the first time
or breaking up for the fourth time
or thinking of him all the time

But I am
despite my history
free from complexity

Sweet tooth

Honey baby, sweetie pie
your sweet tooth I can't deny
I am your pastry, squeeze out my filling
suck out my cream, and as I keep pouring
my honey, chocolate, caramel skin
will pour across your fruit

Sugar plum
devour every piece, eat every crumb
enjoy my sugar as long as it comes

I am your crème brûlée
ready to serve you wherever you lay
however you like to get fed
whether on the kitchen counter, or in your bed

Honey dip
split me and dip me into your milk
and dip your Oreo into my lips

I am your dessert
sitting in the palm of your hands
this bakery delivers to only one man

Your indulgent nature
is addicted to my sweet
I am your treat

Crazy

My smile smiles every time you smile at me.
I love giving you love until I can't breathe.
I want you to want every piece of me.
Can't you see how breezy our love can be?

I trust that you trust your trust in me.
I'm happy you're happy being happy with me.
I laugh at all the laughs you've laughed with me.
Can't you see how silly our love can be?

I see what you see in me.
I wish exactly what you wish to be.
I dream the dreams you dream for me.
Can't you see how easy our love can be?

I cry every time your cries cry out to me.
My screams scream every time you scream at me.
I hate having to hate you every time you hate me.
Can't you see how angry our love can be?

I forgive you for giving me so much strain.
I think that you think our love is insane.
I love how you love me all the same.
Can't you see how crazy our love can be?

Timeless Love

My timeless love,
how you heal and let me love again
how you set time to perfect
to you and me in an infinite space in time

My timeless love,
let's live life like it doesn't last forever
let's love like love only comes around once
in a life-time is on our side
from sunset to sunrise
let's stay up all night
and do the timeless act of love

My timeless love,
do not fear the future
please, don't rush
for only time will tell
what love has for us

Brand New

I wish I knew,
that old love could act so brand new
I came to realize
that everything you told me were lies
a temporary truth, Ruth
Ruthless were your tactics to lay me down
just to let me down

I wish I knew,
that old love could act so brand new
the sweetest poison, the oldest remedy
creating concoctions to formulate
and convince the innocence of my heart
to fall in love with the vulnerability known as us

I believed it, and I screamed it
ran around so everyone could see it
running down to the masses
telling everyone I needed it
how I needed you,
just to find out that you weren't true
I wish I knew,
That old love could act so brand new

Is Love

I blow you a kiss and make you drool with desire
hold your hand and make your palms perspire
one kiss on the cheek and you'll be in a daze
perfume on your sheets has you dreaming for days
but calm down, baby, no need to rush
because all we're feeling is lust

Looking back I've seen how much we've grown
with time, our story has been told
this is no longer a teenage crush
and what we're feeling isn't lust

I've cried on your shoulder a million times
through the years you've stood by my side
so come on baby, we've waited long enough
and what we're feeling is love

For Now

I wanted to be in love
but instead
I'm in a relationship

I wanted some time
and you gave me a lot
of flowers and gifts instead

I wanted intimacy
but instead
you offered me security

For all I wanted
I got you
and that's all I need
for now

My Ending

Love is the most universal thing we have
for every story seems to be themed in its honor
and though I may not understand it in practice
I do in theory

For whether it be a state of being
In love is a wonderful place to be
or it be an action
we all want to be loved
or maybe just a losing game
we're all doomed to play

I can't help but wonder
what will be my story
of this thing called love
and what will be
my ending

Best With You

Baby tell me what's a girl to do
when the worst for me is the best with you

The way you kiss me when you miss me
makes me want you to miss me everyday
and every day I come home cranky and tired
you rub my shoulders, my back, and my feet
how is it when I'm angry you can stay so sweet?

Baby tell me what's a girl to do
when the worst for me is the best with you

The way we make up when we argue
makes me want to argue every night
the way you hold me when I'm cold
makes me want to be cold all the time
and every time I get a cold
you're there to console me

Baby tell me what's a girl to do
when the worst for me is the best with you.

The way you spoil me when we're broke
makes me want to be broke all the time
and all the times you made me hotdogs and chips
are the most romantic nights we spent

Baby tell me what's a girl to do
when the worst for me is the best with you.

Believe

You gave me all I ever needed
and I gave you my all
you made me believe in you
baby you made me believe

I gave you all I had to offer
loyalty and love
I gave you time as you did me
you made me believe in us
baby you made me believe

A common man, a common deed
can do the greatest things
I made you believe in me
baby I made you believe

The youngest love has so much promise
neither you nor I can see
I made you believe in us
baby I made you believe

Bring Me Back

I could write a poem, draw a picture or two
but that won't bring me you
sculpt the moments that we shared together
but that won't bring me you

Carry around the things you gave me
remember all the sweet things you told me
but that won't bring me you

Replay all our times together
reread all your old lover letters
but that won't bring me you

Send me gifts, send me flowers
talk to me on the phone for hours
but, baby, that just won't do
because only you
can
bring me back
to you

I Didn't See it Coming

I wonder what happened that day
and I wonder if you saw it happen
for you loved me, unexpectedly
and I didn't even see it coming

The day I loved you in a way
that was healthy for the both of us
the day you loved me in a way
that made me feel healthy
that made me feel loved
ended disaster
ended dismay
Did you see it, baby?

Or did my sight
show you the feeling
and you responded to my love
or did you always
know you'd see
and decided not to look
until that day…

A young lover can never see
the vision of a young dreamer
male and female, respectively
for you loved me, unexpectedly
and I didn't even see it coming

Armor

Can one of you go tell
my knight in shining armor
that I don't need him anymore

While you all told me
since I was eight, to wait
on some man who was going
to help me escape
the reality of life
 I found a man
who's going to make me his wife

Can someone go tell these little girls
to stop looking for a man
in a shiny suit
and shiny things
let them know
sometimes they don't come
on horses
or with a fortune
there's no remorse when
you find a real man
to take your course

Because mine didn't have to come
in a shiny suit or horses
or even a fortune
to give me everything I needed
and everything I wanted
and more

Can someone please go tell
my knight in shining armor
that he's already been replaced
before I even see him
although I was told to wait
to be his princess
a man has made me his queen

Someone please scream
scream out to these little girls
and tell them
a real man
may not sweep you off your feet
he'll help you stand on them

The reality is so much better
than the fantasy
a real man is so much better
than a shiny suit
falling in love is so much better
than the façade of getting rescued

I found my perfect man
and he didn't come
in a shiny suit
or ride up with horses
or even have a fortune
but he gives me
everything I need
everything I want
and more

Perfect

As impossible as it may be
he strived to be perfect just for me
and through the time he tried to be
he became the perfect man for me

Despite the imperfections of me
he saw what I was meant to be
and with love and lust his eyes could see
the perfect girl for him was me

Life

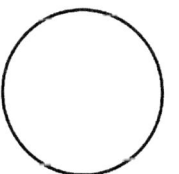

Untraditional

Neither in the office or the kitchen
independence or submission
neither suit nor skirt
but floating somewhere in between
was the plan
how untraditional, I am

For those not for the 9 to 5
enjoys the element of surprise
no routine dream was in my plan
how untraditional, I am

The economy does not give way
for all those looking for a 2 week pay
owning my own was in my plan
how untraditional, I am

Hold your Opinion

I will not apologize for eating watermelon
or being able to cook fried chicken
next time, hold your opinion
because I got culture in my kitchen

So Italians can eat pasta
Mexicans make tacos
Spanish create tapas
but you put black face on every woman
who's in movies and shows doing soul food cooking
who are you to make a mockery of my history
next time, hold your opinion
because I got flavor in my kitchen

If you insist on demeaning it
why do you keep on eating it?
last time I checked we cooked for you
for hundreds of years
from my ancestor's hands you fed your kids
and from what was left we had our meals
from whatever we could pluck, boil, or peel
next time, hold your opinion
because I got history in my kitchen

The way my children smile when dinner is served
Husband walks through the door, my meal is preferred
3 generations over one pot, much is learned
Next time, hold your opinion
Because I got family in my kitchen

For all you vegetarians,vegans, and "I don't eat a lot"s
I got greens and lima beans in my pot
I have no issue with healthy living
I just make sure there's something good in it
Next time, hold your opinion
Because I got real food in my kitchen

Never be the End

Goodnight, dear friend
because our goodnight
will never be the end
home for the holidays, as I see you smiling, Hi
because when the holidays come, so do I
so we never say goodbye

We never have to wait,
or it's never too late
to celebrate a birthday
365 days sounds good
for it covers the range
of time to choose
to celebrate with you
goodnight, dear friend
because our goodnight
will never be the end

No Catholic blood is needed
for a Mardi Gras adventure
Cinco de Mayo will still be fun
with no travel across the border
whatever day that I may comeback
we'll make time for all of that
no matter the occasion
there is something to do
some trouble for us to get into
just me and you
goodnight, dear friend
because our goodnight
will never be the end

Color Blind

Why must you forget that I'm black,
to remember that I'm human
or that I'm a woman

Thank you, America, for Affirmative Action
for that box I have to check
that says non-Hispanic African-American Black
and note how race won't affect my employment
thank you for reminding me
that you're trying not to notice
that I'm black
to remember that I'm human
or that I'm a student

Our demise is our compromise
to find
there's no such thing as color blind

Why do only people who are clear, beige, or white
like to describe me as articulate
or well spoken
thank you for forgetting
that you trying not to notice
that I'm the token
as in black
to remember that I'm human

Our demise is our compromise
to find
there's no such thing as color blind

Thank you to all the men
who described me as the most beautiful
black woman they've ever seen
although somewhat demeaning
thank you for remembering
that I'm black
on top of a woman
to forget that I'm human

And no recruiter, I won't sue you
for not giving me the job
do you think that I was robbed?
was it hard to realize
that I'm human
while still being black
and a woman

Our demise is our compromise
to find
there's no such thing as color blind

Once Lived

Time will never be repeated
for the life once lived, yet twice defeated

What would you do if you weren't afraid?
for contentment is the mark of failure
with fear comes the death of a man
hesitation births the uncertain
and breeds the unsuccessful

Time will never be repeated
for the life once lived, yet twice defeated

What would you do if you only lived once?
many men have been defeated
not from loss or disappointment
but simply because they never tried something
never fought for anything

Time will never be repeated
for the life once lived, yet twice defeated

Didn't roll the dice, yet lost the game
Lost the fight and didn't take one blow
No second chances, no revisions
You have to use the time you're given
Let this be a calling, the awakening of you

Time will never be repeated
For the life once lived, yet twice defeated

A Book Called Perfect

I'm looking for a book called perfect
have you seen it?
everyone is referring to it
it talks about the body, the life,
how to make a living
and I need to know if I'm fitting
the guidelines

Social stigmas, cultural influences
individual ideologies
have caused more interpretations
than the bible
of the word, perfect.

I think it's about time
that we agree to disagree
on the word, the body, the life,
the way I say potato
when I can wear white
when I can do what
at which age
who I marry
or don't
age
sex
location

Let happy be my perfect
Let content be my perfect
Let my journey be my perfect
and I'll let you go
and choose yours

America

I scream for the voiceless
I see for the blind
marching to glory leaving no one behind

I reach out to the homeless
I cry for the lost
fighting for justice no matter the cost

I pray for the forgotten
I stand for the poor
honoring those that came before
they, too, are America.

Sees Me

I see the sky
And the sky sees me
It has freckles just like me
I see the smoke and smoke sees me
I exhale and it's free like me
I see sleep and sleep sees me
I go to sleep and it dreams like me
I see the sun and the sun sees me
I wake up and so does he

Disappointments

If you sit and wait for your dream, it will come
and pass you by
because dreams don't come from sitting

If you wish for love, it will come
and break your heart to pieces
be careful what you wish for

If you call and pray to God, he'll come
not when you call
but he's always on time

The Part of Me

The part of me inside of you
will always remember us
the right now in tomorrow
will never let me forget my past
your love in this chaos
will always make me happy
the pavement in my path
will never let me forget my steps

Consequences

I will cry over you when I miss you
I will bury you when you are dead
so don't break my heart until you know
you'll never wish to hold it again

Be careful with what you're doing
please, watch what you say
tomorrow is determined
by your actions, today

Jasmine

They see me, blooming
and they stop to notice me

They see my colors brightening the sun
and they stop in awe of my beauty

They see me rise, kissing the sky
and they stop and gaze at my size

They see me dancing against the wind
and they stop to see my movement

They see the rain pouring down on me
and they stop to admire my growth

Bittersweet

When I left, my heart grew weary
and my soul wandered endlessly
I tucked my life in close
engulfed in the world around me
but this is what I wanted
a fresh start…a new end

Caught in the liminality
a mélange of adulthood and confusion
lost in a world of drinking
running to a class after a night I don't remember
cultural awkwardness and regional tension
midterms and campaigns, grades and labels
I reign

But the perfection of high school still haunts me
like a fantasy that keeps playing in my thoughts
a dream that I wake up from day after day after
all of the tantrums, and teachers and text messages,
dresses, detentions, bad hair days, breakups,
makeups, movie nights, and fights
I'd do it all over again

So Easy

Why is it so easy
to tell them what to do
instead of doing it for you

The way you pour water in a plant
instead of drinking it

The way you talk healthy
instead of being it

Feed your dog organic food
instead of eating it

Why is it so easy
to tell them what to do
instead of doing it for you

Give advice on life
but you never lived it

Read the word
and never depict it

Encouraged a dream
but you never pursued it

Why is it so easy
to tell them what to do
instead of doing it
for you

Nothing More

Nothing more than an addiction you're trying to quit
nothing more than that dress you just can't fit
nothing more than not being able to pay rent
and nothing less, will cause you stress

Nothing more than a boss you're trying to impress
nothing more than an all-nighter right before a test
nothing more than a noise when you're trying to rest
and nothing less, will cause you stress

Nothing more than a man that'll drive you crazy
nothing more than having an unexpected baby
nothing more than any burden that you may carry
and nothing less, will cause you stress

But I'm not stressed
I'm too blessed
(nothing more, nothing less)
to be stressed

Insatiable

When we have something, we want everything
when we have nothing, we want anything
but as soon as we get anything, we want it all
and if we do get everything,
we're sad because we don't have anyone
as soon as we get someone, nothing else matters
until they leave us, with nothing.

Pursuing happiness is often times pursuing money
but everyone is out to get your money
or you, for your money
leaving you to pursue the one thing most vital:
Happiness

Mirror, Mirror

Today, I looked into the mirror
and stared into my eyes
my big, brown, beautiful eyes
and I said, God.Girl you're gorgeous.
you should be having men wanting to shower you
with diamonds and Porsches.

I'm sorry, that's just me being cocky.
would you like me better?
if I talked about how I went to college
and got fatter. No, I won't do that anymore

I looked in the mirror and got hooked on me.
look at this great beauty, girl look at your booty
lol…I had to laugh.
I never use to talk like this in the past.
until I looked in the mirror
and spotted my hourglass
and I can see you thinking
I can't stand her cocky ass.

And that's fine. Because tomorrow, I'm going to
look into the mirror, and stare into my eyes.
and this time I won't act surprise, when I realize
how beautiful I am.
all you other women are waiting around for a man,
to tell you the same thing that
I'm telling myself now. You want to love yourself?
well I'm going to tell you how
just look in the mirror.

Progress

Are you mad?
because I speak with conviction
and who I am does not fit
your one dimensional description
surprised when I'm the doctor
filling out the prescription
and when we make a decision
we don't ask for your permission

Are you angry?
because when I walk into a room
my head is not down
and I step into a place
where you think I'm not allowed
or I'm too loud,
too black, too proud
I'm not your average token
peppered in a crowd

Are you indignant?
because I walk with a swagger
and every semester your school gets blacker
and every year we smash the statistics
we don't bother with you'll
because we have our own business

Are you uncomfortable?
Because your daughter has a daughter
with kinky locks
And every time you turn around
there's a new Negro on your block
Or it's only ten o'clock.
And you already saw ten positive
black people on FOX

You see, while you were worked into this
classist, racist, process
Black people got together and we
made a little progress

Crabs in a Barrel

Your negativity tickles me
your middle school ridicule has no effect on me
but still I see,
you try to break me down day after
day after all that I done been through
what makes you think I'd even acknowledge you?

I done won too many battles to battle with you
I've overcome too many trials to go to trial with you
I've made too many mistakes to make a mistake out
of you.

What I've come to find is only hurt people,
hurt people
now who's to blame for your pain, I can't say.
but I appreciate all of you, anyway.

Oya

O yes, Oya. O yes, Oya is me.
and if you cannot see, it's because
my burgundy coins and purple majesties
are all bowing down to me
royalty, your majesty
the beginning and the end of this hierarchy

I'm the one that makes the River Niger flow
I'm the one that makes the grass and the trees
and the roots and the new fruits grow.
I'm the one that Shango took to battle
and all his other wives don't matter
all Oshun ever did was lay on her back
and on top of that
all Oba ever did was cut off her ear

O yes, Oya. O yes, Oya is me.
and if you cannot hear, it's because
I'm the one that makes the hurricanes
and tornadoes roar
I'm the one that cuts off stagnation
so there can be more and more

O yes, Oya. O yes, Oya is me.
and if you cannot breath, it's because
I'm the one that rocks the old to sleep
I'm the one that has their soul to keep
I'm the one that guards them into the next life
and make sure they're all right
and they're all right
O yes, Oya. O yes, Oya is me.

If Tomorrow Doesn't Come

If tomorrow doesn't come, I came today
and it rained today, and I soaked it up
threw it back at the sun
and let it run down my skin

If the sun doesn't come tomorrow, it came today.
and I played today, in its brown skin rays
In my brown skin days, I've been sun kissed
and if that was my last kiss, I've been kissed today

And if the sun doesn't come
and the rain doesn't fall
If tomorrow doesn't come
I've had my fun
I've already won
today

Myself

I'd rather rebel against you
than myself
I'd rather deny you
all the greatness of me
than to deny myself

For me, I cannot lie to
for me, I cannot go from
for you may never have
this battle
for I, will always win
for I, will always choose myself

Footsteps

Listen to me
never let your family,
determine your destiny
my mother's mistakes
doesn't determine my heartaches
and my heart aches for all those girls
that fall into the footsteps
of every mistake, misfortune, and misdemeanor
made by their mothers and never once thought
they could break the chain

My father's choices doesn't set my misfortune
and it's unfortunate that some fall into the footsteps
of every fault, frustration, and failure made
by their fathers and never once thought
they could break the chain.
Listen to me
never let your family,
determine your destiny

Just Your Taste

Excuse me…
were you speaking to me?
I didn't know my name was
aye girl, hey shorty, sexy little cutie in the red shirt
and when you start to flirt,
I didn't need to know that
long hair, big booty, slim waist was just your taste

It was a waste of time to hear your line of
Aye baby let me take you out
but I have to pick him up at his mama's house.

Then you ask for my number, when you can see me
can you come over, where you can find me
If I say no, you'll just talk to
the girl walking behind me
miss aye girl, hey shorty, sexy little cutie
in the red shirt
long hair, big booty, slim waist
who is just your taste

I Capture My Beauty

I capture my beauty, so when it fades away
my words will be here to stay

I capture my eyes as they captivate all
slanted brown beauties eyelashes cascading tall

I capture my cheeks with round satisfaction
high boned, peeked, and red with compassion

I capture my skin, freckled perfection
bright undertone and peanut butter complexion

I capture my shape, an hourglass distinction
curvaceous escape, a divine creation

I capture my beauty, so when it fades away
my words will be here to stay

Be a Magnet

Be a magnet for love,
Be a magnet for peace
what you fail to realize
is that you attract what you keep
inside; greed, sorrow and pride
you let it come in you
instead of letting it die, it rebirths
and it's that thing that makes you curse
makes you angry, makes you ignorant,
makes you worse

You console it, you mold it, and you hold it
inside you, so you draw it to you
things happening to you because you choose it
you're a magnet for it
you're the ring bearer for it
crowned with a frown
and the fact is, you attract it
a slave for it

You let it manifest in your chest
and you birth it, you breast feed it
because you need it to grow
so you can blame someone else
for why you didn't get where you wanted to go
but what you fail to realize
is that you reap what
you sow

So be a magnet for change
the words you said yesterday

today, you don't have to swallow
don't let it follow you for the rest of your life
don't let the past, last until today

So be a magnet for progression
be a magnet for change
be a magnet for the movement
be a magnet for the magnificent

Demand you happiness
freedom, destiny
be a magnet for that

For the innocence of forgiveness
for the comfort of compassion
be a magnet for love

Let it wallow in your spirit
let it captivate your soul
let it embody your nature
as you grow old

Whatever you want
demand for it, stand for it
think it and speak it
make it become your life

Be the ring bearer for that
crown yourself with that

Be a Magnet
Be a Magnet
Be a Magnet
for that

Everybody Knows

Everybody knows, everybody knows
but the one who's suppose to know
our minds go as far as our eyes will believe
being naïve may deceive
even the brightest human beings
everybody knows, everybody knows
but the one who's suppose to know

The "he said she said' at its best
the rumors at its worst
the confusion at its first
everybody knows, everybody knows
the truth

The girl who says he's not cheating
the boy who brags on his up-and-coming career
the woman who thinks her child is eating
the man that believes he has nothing to fear
everybody knows, everybody knows
but the one who's suppose to know

Everybody is anybody who knows their own truth
or the whole truth
nothing but the person who's suppose to know,
knows
everybody knows
but you

Hate to Love You

Money
I hate to love you
I love to spend you
I love to make you
it's hard to save you

I'm so confused
why we make so many decisions
based on you
like family, love, happiness
peace, my health, convenience
sanity, travel, location
and all logical aspects of life
goes out the window
with the mere mention
of your name

Money
I'm so confused
it's hard to save you
I love to make you
I love to spend you

I hate everything about
loving you
What have you made of us?
workaholics, shady occupations
late night, weekend, holiday workers
isolated individuals, untrustworthy negotiators
Money

finding the balance
between making
and saving
and spending you
creating my
indifferent disposition towards you
is where I find my peace with you
Money

Comfort

I am my own comfort
rocking back and forth in my arms
I stoke my hair and wipe my tears

Wrapped in my own idea of contentment
soothed by my own sweet words
my own protector, my own provider
I am my own comfort

Diamonds and Pearls

Boys use to grow up to be men
then someone put that to an end
he said, be a woman, wear diamonds and pearls
who will be left for the little girls?

Should they go white? Would that be wrong?
or spend each night alone
alone with their diamonds, alone with their pearls
who will be left for the little girls?

Should they turn to each other? Because you did too
because all the boys are saved for you
saved with your diamonds, saved with your pearls
who will save the little girls?

Order My Steps

If you gave me love, would I refuse it?
Offered me happiness, would I choose it?

Gave me power, would I abuse it?
If I had everything, would I lose it?

Lord, I know it's not my time
but when it is, what will I do with it?

Reign over kingdoms, will I lead them?
Service the poor, would I feed them?
Lectured the youth, would I teach them?

Lord, I have a lot of life left
but when it comes
please order my steps.

This is All I Need

Sometimes, this is all I need
eating popcorn, watching T.V.
laughing in my sweats
lets do this again, my friend
sometimes this is all I need

A sip of wine, an easy night
drifting into the music
lets do this again, my friend
sometimes this is all I need

Family night on a random day
not doing much at all
next week? Count me in
sometimes this is all I need.

Laying in bed, pillow talking
candle light into the night
I can do this again, my friend
sometimes this is all I need.

Little Old Me

One day I hope to die of old age
how wonderful it would be
to fall asleep, one warm summer night
happy, little old me.

No cancer, no disaster
no health complaints from me
just close my eyes and drift away
how beautiful that would be
laying there in my bed
happy, little old me

Many are scared to think about
the day that they might leave
afraid of all the horror stories
their minds could conceive
but there will be no horror stories
no hospital bed for me
just laying down in my warm bed
happy, little old me

Oh how peaceful
it will be
to close my eyes
and drift away
happy, little old me.

Family

Have You Ever Been a Kid?

Did you ever wish upon a star
and hope it would come true?
Have you ever looked up in the sky,
and wonder how long it's been blue?

Have you ever been so happy
thinking the world revolved around you?
Have you ever dreamed of lollipops
chocolate and gumdrops too?

Have you ever found joy, in tying your shoe?
In trying something new? in just being you?

Have you ever been called goofy, silly, or wild?
Did you ever, were you ever,
have you ever been a child?

Did you ever see a bird fly away
and wonder where it went?
Have you ever heard of love and romance
and wondered what it meant?

Did you ever want a pony,
Barbie or a Ken?
Did you ever find joy
when you first could count to ten?

Have you ever been in trouble
and you did't know what you did?
Did you ever, were you ever,
have you ever been a kid?

It's All for a Reason

It's all for a reason, it's all for a way
I'm mama's little angel and I'm here to stay
although I'm only ten
mama teaches me about you
I'd be like you, Lord, everyday
If only, if only I could
I wouldn't lie, I wouldn't cheat
not even would I curse
but every day, Lord, everyday
it seems I'm getting worse

Sometimes I scream, sometimes I'm mean
I'm a little, no very, unfaithful
skipping class, making my mama mad
I'm a little, no very, ungrateful

What if I decide to devote my life to you?
Would you forgive me for my sins or at least a few?
What if I say I'm sorry for as long as I live?
Will you send me to heaven and decide to forgive?

It's all for a reason, it's all for a way
since you've done so much for me
I'll be with you to stay

I stand like a tree, as he does for me
until the storm passes me by
for everything he tells me to do
I surely will do it
although I'm in a storm
I know you'll bring me through it

sometimes it's hard believing in you
but everything you've told me, I know that it's true
it's all for a reason, it's all for a way
and as I'm growing I'll be with you to stay

Now I'm trying to tell this daughter of mine
how you've picked me up and allowed me to shine
I tell her in life things may go wrong
and only through you she can be strong
although I'm not perfect, I try and I try
to reach her your way, make sure she stays with you
ease her woes, make sure she knows you're true

It's all for a reason, Lord I'm on my way
and when I go to heaven my angel will have to stay

My Grandmother

I love my grandmother
More and more each day
I love her fresh pot of greens
And her sweet potato pie
I love her swing low sweet chariot
And her Billy Holiday blues
More and more each day

I love her stories of kings and crowns
And slaves and civil rights
I love her poise, posture
And presence in a room, more and more each day

I love her midnight snacks
And her thanksgiving meals
I love her spirit, more and more each day

I love the pride in her work
The strength of her soul
I love the bareness of her feet
the wisdom in her words, more and more each day

I love the truth in her eyes
And the joy in her smile
She loves her family, more and more each day

I love her faith in God
And her comforting arms
I love her sacrifices
More and more each day,
I love my grandmother

Always

I thought I was so grown
by the age of three
because the whole world revolved around me
but only when I was with my dad
I'll always be his baby girl.

I thought I was so grown
when I use to back talk my mom
and both my parents had to keep me in line
my mama said I had a mouth just like my dad
I'll always be his baby girl.

I thought I was so grown
when I got some attention
I got a couple awards and accreditation
at the end of the day, I'm just happy to make my dad proud
I'll always be his baby girl.

I thought I was so grown
when I started dating
then realized it was overrated
because the only man that won't disappoint me is my dad
I'll always be his baby girl.

I thought I was so grown
when I went to school
until I saw how this world could be so cruel
the only person that'll take care of me is my dad
I'll always be his baby girl.

I thought I was so grown
when I got perfect grades
but it's all credited to how I was raised
all these years my dad pushed me
I'll always be his baby girl.

I thought I was so grown
but it use to drive me crazy
he always told me to eat, act, and dress like a lady
now I'm a class act, because of my dad
I'll always be his baby girl.

I thought I was so grown
even when I made a mistake
at times I did more than my parents could take
but my dad forgave me, every time he told
I'll always be his baby girl.

I thought I was so grown
because he never beat me
I think it was because I was such a sweetie
but my dad still threatens to use that belt because
I'll always be his baby girl.

I thought I was so grown
because I've been treated like royalty
all through my life, he spoiled me
my dad can't even hide how much he loves me
I'll always be his baby girl.

I thought I was so grown
in so many ways
whether I am or not I know to this day
if nothing else is true in this world
I'll always always always
be my daddy's baby girl.

25th Anniversary

In 1982, on August seventh
a church in St. Louis had a beautiful wedding
Johnny and Minga were joined together
to a marriage that seems to have lasted forever
25 years. And from what I know
there are 25 more to go.

Love and marriage are not the same
marriage takes commitment, conflict, and change
through all of the triumphs and hardships you face
marriage reminds you
why you fell in love in the first place
25 years. And from what I know
there are 25 more to go.

The word sacrifice
doesn't begin to describe parenthood
children don't appreciate
their parents like they should
between love, money, time and energy
there's a lot to give
thank God you have someone
to raise your children with
25 years. And from what I know
there are 25 more to go.

You two have stood the test of time
together you've shared half of your lives
a long lasting marriage is extremely rare
with all of the memories and laughter you share
25 years. And from what I know
there are 25 more to go.

You are the few that practice what you preach
you are the change that we all seek
for all that you've given, for all that you do
with much gratitude we bow to you
25 years. And from what I know
there are 25 more to go.

A Newborn Mother

And you were amazing
as I saw your first breath
as I saw your eyes as they cried out for my attention
a flashback of your father's first moment with me
your first moment with me
is God's most imitating gift
the gift of life
mother and wife
and I laugh as your eyes look of wonder
and I wonder if you're wondering who I am
your mother and I wonder
who you'll be and what you'll see
where will you go, how fast you'll grow
then you have another little brother
I feel the fear, excitement, mystery, and joy
of a new born mother

I Just Can't Tell It All

Who can compare?
to the woman who raised me,
but never was afraid to spank me
who can compare?
to the woman who changed my diapers,
put me in my clothes
put barrettes in my hair
and wiped my nose

                      I just can't tell it all

Who can compare?
to the woman who taught me how to read
taught me how to tie my shoes, and my abcs
Who can compare?
to the woman who loved me
loved me so much, she couldn't love me anymore
loved me so much

                      I just can't tell it all

Who can compare?
to my inspiration, whose preparation
gave me everything I ever needed to succeed
beyond even my own dreams
Who can compare?
to the woman who saved me from myself
and everything else this world can throw at you

who showed me the true meaning of I love you unconditionally
                        I just can't tell it all

Who can compare?
to the woman who took me to church
took me to Africa and Europe
and back, took me to practice, rehearsal
eye doctor, nail place, hair shop
                        I just can't tell it all

Who can compare?
to the woman who forgave me
every time I did something wrong
                        I just can't tell it all.
Who can compare?
to the woman who gave me life
a mother, a sister, a daughter, a wife

a homemaker, a caregiver, a child of God
                        I just can't tell it all.

About The Author

Jasmine Furr was born in Atlanta, GA to Minga and Johnny Furr. She grew up in St. Louis, Missouri living with her parents and grandparents all under one roof. Jasmine began her love for poetry in middle school when she picked up a poetry book written by Nikki Giovanni. That Christmas, her mother bought her a notebook and encouraged her to write a few poems of her own. It is in that purple notebook that Jasmine wrote all of the poems featured in *Unexpected Moments: a collection of poems on love, life and family*. Publishing her debut book in 2011, Jasmine looks forward to sharing her poetry with you for many years to come.

Untraditional Publishing Company, LLC is the official publishing company of *Unexpected Moments: a collection of poems on love, life, and family*. To order books, or for publishing services, feel free to contact us.

UntraditionalPublishing.com

UntraditionalPublishing@gmail.com

@UntraditionalCo